Khalid Abdalla

Nowhere

An Anti-Biography

Salamander Street

PLAYS

First published in 2024 by Salamander Street Ltd., a Wordville imprint. (info@salamanderstreet.com).

Nowhere © Khalid Abdalla, 2024

Cover photograph by Manuel Vason.

ISBN: 9781068696251

10 9 8 7 6 5 4 3 2 1

Further copies of this publication can be purchased from www.salamanderstreet.com

Wordville

Beyond right and wrong, there is a field.
I'll meet you there.

INTRODUCTION BY RUTH LITTLE

utopia (N.)
1551, from Modern Latin Utopia, literally "nowhere".

Nowhere is not a play. It's not an autobiography, a political history, a work of physical theatre or an installation. Its origin is in an idea fashioned by empire and its 20th-century offspring into a state of being as arbitrary as the nation state. The state of nowhere is the invisible terrain to which millions dispossessed by violence and corruption are forced to claim citizenship while awaiting return to their homelands, to the restoration of those lands as home, places of dwelling, participation, belonging.

Negative definition is the rhetorical weapon of power: the 'dis' in dispossessed, the 'illegal' attached to the immigrant, the invisibility of the poor, the silence that surrounds the sayable and thinkable.

Nowhere is a story in search of itself, which, in the process of searching, becomes a story of us all.

Khalid Abdalla is a Glasgow-born British-Egyptian son, husband, father, writer, actor and activist whose life is a node in a global web of interdependence, joined by supple threads to friends, allies, artists, but at the same time subject to sticky entanglement in the operations of power and capital.

The work's seeming slippages and tonal shifts constantly alter the aperture of our understanding, from the local and personal to the global and political, until we come to know, beyond right and wrong, that we are all, to different degrees, being *danced* even as we make our own joyous dances. And this knowledge, created in the place of this performance, is also the foundation of human community, of an intimacy and vulnerability—and responsibility— that offers hope at the same time as insisting, *insisting*, that for many the rhyme of history imposes its patterns so much more violently on some bodies than on others. But Khalid will not let us look away. And he doesn't seek to divide, but to create a felt sense of how colonial histories magnify and intensify inequality over time, until difference comes to seem complete and naturalised, and therefore unassailable.

Against the odds, *Nowhere* asserts the tenacity of insight, anger, creativity and hope in response to injustice. It is an 'antibiography', a work of refusal: refusal of isolation, ignorance, anaesthesia, overwhelm. A 'no' to 'nowhere'. But refusal demands its opposite for the sake of change. *Nowhere* is also an adamant 'Yes' manifesto. *Yes* to the truth and humbling implications of complexity, to the right to association, to play and mourning, ritual and testimony. Yes to self among selves, to the unfraying selvedge edge of the weave, to the warp and woof of being whole, together. Despite suppression and surveillance selvedge—the prescriptive stamp in the passport, the segregation at the border— the will to belong stirs like a bird and cannot, forever, be silenced. *Nowhere* insists, above all, that to truly see ourselves and one another, we must learn to see differently, to move differently, to be differently moved, in places like this, which are nowhere and everywhere.

Ruth Little
2024

ACKNOWLEDGEMENTS

Perhaps above all this play is in search of a space of belonging, and in the absence of a world in which we can safely gather and thrive beyond the fractures of displacement, prison, war and various forms of exile in body, space and time, there are those who have helped me find the space *Nowhere* is searching for, in their homes, their conversations, their parties, their collaborations, their friendship and their love. The words I have found and the production of this play would not have been possible without Aalam Wassef, Aya Wassef, Ayyam Sureau and Habiba Hassan-Wassef, the Association des Amis d'Aalam and the friends themselves; as well as the following people and the constellations around them: Tamer El Said, Aura Satz, Mazen Kerbaj, Tala Hadid, Chris Thorpe, Ruth Little, Alberto Ferro, Shane Scott, Kerry Wilde, Philip Swan, Cat Villiers, Paul Greengrass, Salam Yousry, Ghalia Benali, the Mosireen Collective, Cimatheque, Brad Butler, Noor Afshan Mirza and James Holcombe of the original no.w.here, Yasmin El-Rifae and Omar Hamilton at Palfest, Nour Abuzaid and Eyal Weizman at Forensic Architecture, the Centre for Systemic Constellations, Led By Donkeys, Simon McBurney, Theatre de Complicite, and everyone on Mnemonic; the teams at the BAC, at HOME, and Salamander Street, the Superheroes and Milan Mezei, Luz Acevedo, Imogen Sarre, Tor Belfrage and everyone at JBA. To my family, my parents and my sister Hanan, I can only say that every word of this play is searching for a way to thank you and show my love. And Cressida, I hope the generations that follow us will find us both somewhere here. You heard every word first, and you are woven in just as we are in Nawar and Aya.

To Kate McGrath, Omar Elerian, all my collaborators and everyone at Fuel, Nowhere is yours, but still my debt of gratitude is overwhelming.

May the parts we carry for each other always find space to dance towards a better future.

Khalid Abdalla

2024

Nowhere was commissioned and first produced by Fuel at Battersea Arts Centre on 1 October 2024 in a production directed by Omar Elerian, funded by Arts Council England and CVC, and supported by Battersea Arts Centre. The production subsequently opened at HOME, Manchester on 22 October 2024.

Writer & Performer	**Khalid Abdalla**
Director	**Omar Elerian**
Set & Costume Designer	**Ti Green**
Lighting Designer	**Jackie Shemesh**
Sound Designer	**Panos Chountoulidis**
Video Designer	**Sarah Readman**
Choreographer	**Omar Rajeh**
Dramaturg	**Ruth Little**
Writing Mentor	**Chris Thorpe**
Associate Director	**Riwa Saab**
Associate Set & Costume Designer	**Jida Akil**
Associate Lighting Designer	**Rajiv Pattani**
Associate Video Designer	**Virginie Taylor**
Video Consultant	**Hanan Abdalla**
Local Engagement Specialist (London)	**Samia Djilli**
Local Engagement Specialist (Manchester)	**Abir Tobji**
Press Representative	**Bread & Butter PR**
Marketing Consultant	**Stacy Coyne Wright**
Poster Photography	**Manuel Vason**
Poster Design	**CHILL Create**
Trailer	**Jamie Isbell/Jam + Post**
Production Manager	**Milorad Zakula**
Company Stage Manager	**Meg Hodgson**
Technical Stage Manager	**Rachel Bowen**

CREATIVE TEAM

Khalid Abdalla | Writer & Performer

Khalid Abdalla is an actor, producer, writer and filmmaker. *Nowhere* is his first play. He is known most notably for his performances in *The Crown* as Dodi Fayed, Marc Forster's *The Kite Runner*, and in the Paul Greengrass features *United 93* and *Green Zone*. He produced and starred in the Egyptian feature *In the Last Days of the City*, directed by Tamer El Said, and in Tala Hadid's *The Narrow Frame of Midnight*, and appears in Jehane Noujaim's Oscar nominated documentary about the 2011 Egyptian revolution *The Square*. He has recently completed filming on his next role in a remake of *The Day of the Jackal*; and performed in *Mnemonic* with Theatre de Complicité at The National Theatre. Khalid is a founding member of three cultural initiatives in Cairo—Cimatheque, Zero Production and Mosireen. He is also an Honorary Fellow of Queens' College Cambridge. Brought up in the UK to Egyptian parents, Cairo and London are his two cities.

Omar Elerian | Director

Omar Elerian is a freelance director, dramaturg, and theatre-maker. Italian of Palestinian descent, Elerian trained in Italy and then graduated from Lecoq International Theatre School in Paris in 2005. He was the resident associate director at London's Bush Theatre from 2012 to 2019 where he commissioned and directed some of the theatre's most successful shows.

His directing credits include the smash-hit *Misty* by Arinzé Kene (Bush Theatre and West End), *ECHO (Every Cold Hearted Oxygen)* and *NASSIM* by Nassim Soleimanpour (Bush Theatre, Traverse Theatre, and world tour), *Going Through* by Estelle Savasta, and *Islands* by Caroline Horton. His most recent directing credits include *The Return of Danton* and *The Long Shadow of Alois Brunner*, both by Syrian playwright Mudar Alhaggi, (Munich Kammerspiele, Schauspiel Leipzig, Theatre an der Ruhr—Germany); *The Chairs* by Eugene Ionesco (Almeida Theatre); *Two Palestinians Go Dogging* by Sami Ibrahim (Royal Court) and *As You Like It* (Royal Shakespeare Company).

Ti Green | Designer

Recent work includes *The Duchess of Malfi*, *MacBeth* (Shakespeare's Globe), *Dr Semmelweis* (Harold Pinter Theatre, Bristol Old Vic); *Waldo's Circus of Magic & Terror* (Extraordinary Bodies, Bristol Old Vic and Tour); *A Dead Body in Taos* (Fuel, Wiltons); *Touching the Void* (Duke of Yorks, Bristol Old Vic); *Cyrano de Bergerac* (Bristol Old Vic); *Bartholomew Fair* (The Globe); Rogers and Hammerstein's *Cinderella* (Sevenages, Shanghai Culture Square and tour of China); *What Shadows* (Birmingham Rep/Edinburgh Lyceum/The Park London); *The Emperor* (Young Vic/ HOME/TFANA New York); *The Government Inspector* (Birmingham Rep and national tour); *The Funfair* and *Romeo and Juliet* (HOME, MTA winner for Best Design); *Playing for Time* (Sheffield Crucible); *Bright Phoenix* (Liverpool Everyman); *A Christmas Carol* (Birmingham Rep); *Orlando* (Manchester Royal Exchange); *Henry VI parts I, II and III*(The Globe); *Time and the Conways* (Royal Lyceum Theatre Edinburgh/ Dundee Rep, CATS nomination for Best Design); *Unleashed* (Barbican) and *The Resistible Rise of Arturo Ui* (Liverpool Playhouse).

Designs for the National Theatre: *Revenger's Tragedy, The Five Wives of Maurice Pinder, The UN Inspector, Coram Boy* (National Theatre/Imperial Theatre New York, Tony nominations for Best Costume and Set Design). For the RSC: *Richard III, Little Eagles, Coriolanus, Dido Queen of Carthage* and *Julius Caesar*.

Jackie Shemesh | Lighting Designer

Jackie Shemesh is a lighting designer for dance, theatre, opera and performing arts. He teaches and guest lectures at institutions including London Contemporary Dance School, Sadler's Wells Summer University, and Goldsmiths.

Recent credits include; *Ben & Imo, As You Like It*, (Royal Shakspeare Company), *Pandemonium* (Wayward Productions, Soho Theatre), *The Seagull* (Jamie Lloyd Company), *Two Palestinians Go Dogging* (Royal Court Theatre), *The Chairs, Mary Stuart, Parallax* (Almeida Theatre), *White Noise* (Bridge Theatre) *Hansard, Death of England Trilogy* (National Theatre & West End) *Ruination* (Royal Opera House), *L'Orfeo* (Opera North), *The Half God of Rainfall* (Birmingham Rep and Kiln Theatre) *The Beloved, Islands and Misty* (Bush Theatre), *What if Women Ruled the World* and *Ceremony* (Manchester International Festival 2017.)

Panos Chountoulidis | Sound Designer

Panos Chountoulidis is a London-based sound designer, originally from Greece, who works across film, performance and immersive media. With a background in electronic composition, Panos brings a unique musical sensibility to his sound design work, seamlessly blending recorded sounds, synthesised elements and musical components to create distinctive sonic landscapes for each project.

Panos has collaborated with directors, filmmakers and artists both in the UK and internationally. He thrives in collaborative environments, where he can delve into the emotional undertones and conceptual ideas of each piece, and craft sound design elements that amplify them.

Recent projects include *Preemptive Listening*—a feature film by the artist Aura Satz, *Two Islets*—an audiovisual digital work by Hiba Ismail, commissioned for the Diriyah Contemporary Art Biennale 2024, various short films for Tate directed by Antony Badu and *Dream Factory*—an experimental short film by Alex Matraxia.

Sarah Readman | Video Designer

Sarah is a lighting, video and creative captions designer. They are passionate about politics, access and play.

As Creative Captioner and Video Designer: *Duchess of Malfi* (Globe); *Driftwood* (Pentabus); *Galatea* (Wildworks and Marlborough Productions); *A Dead Body in Taos* (Fuel); *The Solid Life of Sugar Water* (Orange Tree): Winner, Best Production (Play) Off-West End Awards, nominated for an Access Offie.

As Video Designer: *Watch on the Rhine* (Donmar); *The Crucible* and *This Beautiful Future* (the Yard Theatre).

As Lighting and Video Designer: *I Wish* (Unicorn); *Endurance* (Jenny Jackson); *Everyman* (Miracle Theatre); *Antigone* (LAMDA); *Midnight Movie* (Royal Court, with Joshua Pharo); *How to Save the Planet* (Unlimited Theatre); *Bystanders* (Cardboard Citizens); *Future Bodies* (RashDash, with Joshua Pharo).

As Lighting Designer: *The Trials and Passions of Unfamous Women* (Clean Break, Lift Festival and Brixton House); *Enitan's Game* (Punchdrunk Enrichment); *Route 158* (Punchdrunk Enrichment); *The Burnt City* (Punchdrunk; As Associate): *Belongings* (Tangled Feet, nominated for TYA

Production at the Offies); *Let Loose* (Unicorn and English National Ballet); *Dirt, WOW EVERYTHING IS AMAZING, Fire in the Machine, Phenomena: a Beginner's Guide to Love and Physics* (Sounds Like Chaos); *Voodoo* (Project O); *punkplay* (Southwark Playhouse).

Omar Rajeh | Choreographer

Omar Rajeh is a choreographer, dancer, founder and artistic director of Maqamat. Initially based in Lebanon since 2002, he moved and set up his company in Lyon in 2020 and he continues to create and develop his projects in Lebanon, France and internationally. He was distinguished by the French Ministry of Culture 'for his contribution and engagement in the service of Culture' with the title of 'Chevalier de l'Ordre des Arts et des Lettres' (Knight of the Order of Arts and Letters).

His more than 20 choreographic creations have been widely presented in major international festivals around the world. His work has always been accompanied by strong compositions and a vigorous physical presence. Omar Rajeh is the founder of the BIPOD—Beirut International Platform of Dance, co-founder of Masahat network, the founder of Takween, an intensive training programme, and Moultaqa Leymoun, a platform that showcases and develops the work of artists and choreographers from the Arab countries. In 2017, he designed and established Citerne Beirut, a choreographic and cultural center in Lebanon which, following its forced dismantling in 2019, gave birth in France to Citerne.live in 2020. omarrajeh.com

Fuel leads the field in independent producing in the UK's live performance sector, working with brilliant artists to explore the big questions of our times, shining a light on how we relate to each other and the world around us, and telling untold stories by under-represented voices. From theatres to car parks, from schools to public spaces, Fuel produces high quality new theatre that reaches diverse audiences across the UK and internationally. Fuel collaborates with outstanding theatre makers with fresh perspectives and approaches who produce shows, performances or experiences which have direct and playful relationships with their audiences.

Fuel is celebrated for its pioneering producing model that develops innovative ideas through attentive collaboration, a spirit of curiosity, and an emphasis on trust. Fuel has developed a reputation for spirited and surprising new theatre, deep relationships with a wide range of artists, and passionate commitment to inclusion and care for young and diverse audiences.

Fuel was founded in 2004 and is led by Kate McGrath. Since its story began, Fuel has produced shows, festivals, films, installations, podcasts, apps and books. In doing so, Fuel has supported the artistic development of over 120 lead artists or companies and reached more than 1.5 million people, live and digitally, hosted over a hundred internships and been recognised with awards for its work. Fuel is currently working with artists and companies including Khalid Abdalla, Will Adamsdale, Jay Bernard, Inua Ellams, Charlie Josephine, Lucian Msamati, Racheal Ofori, Toby Olié, Joelle Taylor, Uninvited Guests and Melanie Wilson. Fuel is supported by Arts Council England as a National Portfolio Organisation, the Esmée Fairbairn Foundation, and the PRS Foundation (Talent Development Network).

fueltheatre.com
Instagram, Facebook, Bluesky, LinkedIn: **@fueltheatre**

Fuel staff

Fuel wishes to thank Lorne Somerville, Pam Vision, Pelin Başaran, Tarek Iskander and all at Battersea Arts Centre, Jennifer Jackson, New Diorama Theatre, Anthony Gray, Stuart Heyes, Shamima Noor, Bernie Whittle, Jack and Zoe Morris, Scarlet McGrath, Vita Morris, Lucy Garcia, Matty Gladstone, Christie Lites, Blue-i, J D McDougall Ltd., European Communication Technology, TripleE Ltd, Green Kit Ltd, Camera House, Lucy Abbotts, Reclaimed & Rustic, Digital Slides, Kate Craddock, Hannah Slimmon, Jennie Gentles, Joy Parkinson, Alex Ward and the team at Here & Now Showcase.

Fuel presents

Nowhere

A new play by Khalid Abdalla

directed by Omar Elerian

A space that presents itself as unmediated. Nothing here wants to hide any more than it already does in the flow of normal life.

There are objects that will be required during the play, but also other objects, on shelves, in drawers. The objects attract attention, and perhaps appear to have a logic. A sense of index, of searching and story. They'll be needed in the play, but not all of them.

There's a table on wheels with gadgets—a visualiser, a laptop, a camera, a midi machine, and a microphone.There might also be some mobile screens, for projecting onto, or screening from. These objects may have something humanoid about them, and can be stood at different heights.

The floor and walls of the theatre will become surfaces for projection, but for now they are just themselves. To the side there are fabrics at different intervals, like curtains, that will be pulled across the space to make more surfaces for projection, and altering the experience of the space. High up there is a mirror ball.

Everyone on entering is given a small 7.5cm square mirror and two pieces of paper in an envelope on which is written: **"Between right and wrong there is a field. I'll meet you there**."

Perhaps like a boat, there is a sense that this space is never still. It is itself by being in movement. And clearly that is about to happen.

However this is interpreted, the set will go on a journey to become something no one at the beginning of the play imagined it would be.

Perhaps the only the figure hiding is the dove.

While every word in this draft has been thought and rethought, please consider the entire script as accurate as you would a medieval map. The territory it is searching for can only be found in actual space, and what becomes of it in time, with other bodies. And so wherever the resonances searched for are enhanced while in process or performance, defer to what is discovered, and what is live.

The opening and ending, in particular, should be open to including deeply felt improvisation, or changes that respond to the state of the world, as well as where, when and with whom the play is being performed.

This draft does not include images, however in performance it is imagined to be rich in sound and images. These should create landscapes that reflect interior states and impulses in the refracted space of a what a theatre can hold. *Nowhere* is in search of what space at its most intense can be.

This text went to press before the end of rehearsals and so may differ slightly from the play as performed.

(Breath)

Hello, good evening and welcome.

Thank you for being the wonderful people crazy enough to want to buy a ticket to nowhere.

If you're someone who has been brought along, and only just found out that nowhere is the name of the show, you might be feeling curious about why someone would call somewhere nowhere.

And the truth is it's the best name I've found for this space we're in now, already appearing more intensely as we shut the doors, *(the doors are shut)* and which I hope to explore with you over the next 80 minutes or so.

It's a space I've reached as the world moves from crisis to crisis to crisis and I eventually reach a point where for me, the stakes have become too high to remain simply as I am out there.

So this shared space is my nowhere, and I'm going to try and go places with you that we often don't out there, in the hope that it might unlock something for us both.

Now, this nowhere is safe, or hopes to be. But there exists a place in the world, now, in which nowhere is safe.

And when nowhere is safe for some people, wherever they are, I believe their nowhere exists for us too.

It enters our world in ways that are intimate, that create a charge around the sayable, a charge around the thinkable, and so what we can discover together.

And when the unfathomable becomes persistent, where do you go?

In the ancient story of the flood, when the entire world is under water, the dove is sent out from the ark to search for land, and finds nowhere to go but the ship from which it came until it's sent out again, and again, and again.

And here we are—a room full of people of varying proximities and distance to world shaping events, in this charge—searching perhaps... and who have found ourselves here.

Take us back to October 6th last year and where were we?

Take us back to September 10th 2001 and where were we?

Some of us here not alive or small children now grown up into this world.

(*Choosing resonantly with the audience*) Perhaps for you it's 1948 or 68 or 82 or 94 or 79, 2008 or 1939.

Where are the traces of the present we carry together?

Which also means where are the other futures?

2011

Sound takes over, and image. Written in Arabic:

The People Demand the Downfall of the Regime

I first shouted these words on January 28th 2011, in a crowd of hundreds of thousands of people marching to take over Tahrir Square, in Egypt.

To enter the feeling of a revolutionary moment, you have to understand the depths of collective penury people were living before it erupted. The suffocation in the certainty of no future, while you live an unbearable present.

The spark came in Tunisia.

(*Some part of this has to be embodied, imagined—the beginning of a physical language that repeats. Perhaps a candle lit.*)

Mohamed Bouazizi, a poor street vendor, already in debt, had his goods confiscated by police, and then he was harassed and humiliated, so then went to complain at the governor's office, where he was refused entry, and so called out...

In Arabic—subtitled: **"If you don't see me, I'll burn myself."**

And so, out on the street, with the words,

In Arabic—subtitled: **"How do you expect me to live?!"**

doused himself in fuel, and set himself on fire.

Millions of people in Tunisia saw him as a reflection of themselves, and rose up in solidarity with his story, demanding change.

And when they toppled their dictator, at first in Egypt, everyone thought, no, it will never happen here.

But then came the call—to congregate and demonstrate—and everyone was shocked by the size.

Out of nowhere, thousands of people discovered they were not alone, and in their scale discovered their power.

So they were swiftly attacked, and Tahrir square emptied.

Jan 25th.

On this day I was in London. I'd just returned after two and half years working on a film called *In the Last Days of the City.* We'd filmed in every demonstration there'd been since 2008.

And so my body was aching to be back in Cairo.

I'm from a family of political prisoners. It goes deep in me.

All I want to know is, are things continuing? Because if people are going out to struggle for this future after they've been attacked, then I know this is real. The signal is this is the time.

And they are.

Maybe only hundreds. But people are fighting. Police are rounding people off the street, simply by listening to their voice.

If it's hoarse, it means you'd been there.

I book my flight.

In the air I look out at London knowing I might never return. I fumble for my phone to take a picture, just as the clouds block the view.

I arrive hours before the entire country is put under curfew.

Then at midnight, internet and mobile networks are shut down.

(Theatre goes dark)

We have nothing left but each other.

In the dark we return to unmediated space.

And in the morning comes the future to which I swear allegiance for the rest of my life.

(Video)

Dictator after dictator is toppled across the region, as the battle for a different world begins.

The future we had told ourselves was impossible is here in front of our eyes.

And we live for it.

—

Until it's pummelled into the shadows.

2013.

I'm in a white room with a curve.

(The space responds in some way)

The ghost of millions marching for a better world still haunts the streets, but no-one dares breach curfew now.

The military is in power, and we're in the aftermath of a massacre.

Over a thousand killed, four thousand injured. Prisons at capacity.

The Muslim Brotherhood were deposed in a popular coup, led by the army.

And now, you're either with us or against us.

The language of binaries has taken over.

How do you speak in this space without going to prison, or having your words co-opted by the two sides you're against?

There are stories of parents informing on their children.

I joke, if they could make breathing illegal they would.

I've given myself over entirely to pro-revolutionary projects, and all of them are now under threat. So, to salvage anything that could have been, I extend myself into timelines that are unlivable.

I'm stuck. Suffocated. Walled in.

And in my tiny apartment I wake up within arms' length of the ceiling staring at a white expanse being attacked by a voice.

You fucking waste of space. What is this bullshit? What the fuck are you doing with your life? Stop fucking around wasting everyone's time with things that are never going to change. This is the way things are. Wake up to the real world, you fucking idiot. Or would you rather be what you always were? Pointless and mediocre. A child. Grow up. What the fuck even... why are you?

And after months of its circling knots, morning after morning, day after day, I wake up one 3am with an absolute fuck it, fuck sleep, fuck this, what is this fucking voice—if I can't sleep him into silence, I'm going to drown him with words I want to hear. I'm going to read all the fucking books that will either send me to sleep or help me understand how this is the actual life we're living and the world outside is so fucking silent.

And now I'm here with you.

In the flow of whatever it is that is happening outside these doors.

Searching for a language, searching for a way to be, that I wouldn't find without friendship.

Because the darkness of the world creates the frame for so much joy.

(Light and dark—a moment of dance—Natascha Atlas—I Put A Spell on You)

If you'd told me ten years ago that I would dance in front of an audience, in something I'd written, I would have thought you were from a parallel universe.

There are people in our lives who help us bridge between who we think we are, and who we want to be.

This is my friend Aalam.

(Image)

A man of parties.

An artist and absurdly creative guy that no matter the darkness of the circumstances could liberate energies that shone a way through.

We met during the heights of the revolution, but really became close when things got bad.

He became like a brother. Someone who could help me find my way when I was lost, and the walls closed in.

Always playful. Always looking for a way out.

(Video of phantom freedom written on wall)

If you can believe it, when he made this video, it was dangerous to do so.

Even during Covid, he created an alter-ego called 'The Balcony Man.'

(Video)

He died recently of pancreatic cancer, and in the year between diagnosis and death really faced the question of how to live when you can't take now or here for granted.

This is from the Facetime we had when he told me about his diagnosis.

What he wanted from us, his friends, was life.

And on every trip I made to see him through the ups and downs of his treatment, I saw him approach his future with an intensity that challenged mine.

As I was looking for ways to be with him when I couldn't, I started a playlist of 'fuck it' and playful energies, called 'Play', and sent it to him for us to collaborate.

When I sent him these messages, I was unsure I'd ever see him again.

(We see a screenshot of the WhatsApp chat:)

A7a this playlist. It's all the stuff "we" have been listening to these past 11 years. It should be called "Us". Thank you Khalid. I'm in between joy and tears—the absolute definition (to me) of joy. (08.24)

I just had a break and listened to your additions. JOY. Joy listening to the songs and hearing you! I LOVE IT!!!! (12.02)

05 Oct 2022

But I did.

During this period, his deepest lifeline was an exhibition of his most recent work, that seemed unlikely to pass.

And so those of us who could, booked our tickets to come in the hope that it would.

The day we arrived he'd just been readmitted to hospital, and fell asleep under force of morphine with two of us in the room, then, by the time he woke up, there were twelve of us around the hospital bed.

Like a miracle he opened his eyes (*looks around*) and said, I have friends.

A few hours later, he created the best party I've ever had. Feeling the rise of energy, as his morphine wore off, he reached for his phone and put on...

(*Music plays*)

This is the rhythm of night

This is the rhythm of my life

—

To the music—a projection display of images, a mix of personal and political. Childhood and formative years interspliced with political events from the UK, the Arab world and elsewhere.

In the performance of the images there is a sense of the furious search for meaning, but also space for others to find themselves. There is pop, and there is politics.

We meet the child Khalid. and we meet his parents. Traveling through the 80s and 90s. A few references to Back to the Future, *and The Libyans moment. Offensive representations of Arabs.*

There can be what appear to be non-sequiturs in the flow of images.

The sequence takes us to 9/11 and the Iraq War.

At which point the music slows down into an evocative slow motion sound.

Reel Bad Arabs *by Jack Shaheen slapped down over the images.*

—

My personal favourite: Disney's *Aladdin* (*Sings*) "Where they cut off your ear if they don't like your face, it's barbaric, but hey, it's home."

Removes photos.

But images are never enough.

*Writes '**Poor You**' under the visualiser.*

Sits in front of a camera and looks at it.

*The words '**Poor You**' are projected above his face.*

These were the first words spoken to me by a casting director in this country.

I sat in front of her, brought in by a friend.

And she looked at my face, just my face, and said, "poor you."

Fight.

Flight.

Or freeze.

I freeze.

I don't remember if she mentions the word terrorism, or terrorist, but it's in the air, as I'm being looked at by an important casting director, lucky, apparently, to be in her presence.

Looking at me. Really thinking.

Then she says, "can you sing?"

The freeze moment repeats.

Of course what you saw in the moments before the freeze, and what you see around it, is the reason two years later I was cast to play the lead hijacker in the film, *United 93*.

It is how I often am in the world.

Sits back in front of the live camera—performing inscrutable tension— perhaps creating a live loop, adding plane sound.

In the context of an imminent hijacking, what is this face hiding?

On all the other planes of 9/11 the hijacking took place within five minutes of the seat belt sign going off, but on *United 93* it took 23 minutes.

Why?

Nobody knows, and I've sat in as close an approximation of that seat as anybody on this earth.

Repeatedly.

In the tension there are questions. Threads. Clues. A whole new world.

Sung—with all the versions on screen making harmonies—a musical screen event that starts simply, or with a piano:

We could spend all evening, speaking of the beauty
Of meeting all the families
Of those who actually died on that plane

We could spend all evening, speaking of the time
of all the love, and all the pain
it actually took, to answer this

Do you think it's possible to do this film correctly?

Perhaps here we see images of the characters Khalid has played in film, each representing a different political trauma—Iraq, 9/11, Afghanistan, Egypt, Dodi & Diana.

Ya aalam, ya aalam

What do you see?

When you look at me?

Poor me

Well that's poor you too

—

Still, at the premiere in New York, five years after the attacks, a short lady comes up to me and slowly, presuming I don't speak English says, I just wanted you to know, I hated you.

And Cressida, my now wife, says to her, "Oh please don't hate him, he's very nice."

So I speak, in this accent, and say, uh… this is my girlfriend, Cressida.

She looks at me stunned.

"You're English?"

She looks at Cressida.

"Where did you meet?"

"Um… at Cambridge."

"Oh… Oh… Well, it's very nice to meet you."

And off she walks into the distance, sipping her champagne.

—

(Scottish accent) And why the hell did you not tell her you're Scottish?

I was born in Glasgow.

(*Scottish accent*) Shut the fuck up. Would you mind if I speak in my actual accent?

I've been locked inside that voice for over 35 years. It's like being occupied by the fucking front bench of Westminster.

Don't get me wrong. I like the intensity, and the soft, gentle charm. But, fuck me, the world's not all so mystically vibrant and dark.

Well, he didn't show you this photo did he?—in all that whatever it was.

Yeah, that's better.

   (*Perhaps a few more photos that bring a different energy.*)

Oh, it feels so good to embarrass him.

Nowhere? Yeah this was Nowhere.

Ohhh, there's lots of detail that he's missed out.

   (*Plays video from first day at school—broad Glaswegian accent*)

So how the hell did they find their way to Scotland?

Well, the man with a moustache is, of course, my father.

Any idea where he was born?

Egypt? No.

America, Urbana Champaign.

(*Switches to American*) Which would make me an American, right?

You see my grandfather was studying for his PhD in Economics at the University of Illinois when my father was born.

(*Switches back to Scottish*) But no, I'm not American. Although, if you ask the Egyptian Government, and this is a true story, (*switches to Irish*) I'm born in Ireland. And the reason for that is that when I went to get my national ID the guy asked me where I was born, and I said Glasgow. He asked where that was, so I said Scotland, and he just couldn't find that on his drop down menu. In Arabic we call the Republic of Ireland, Irelanda El Horra, which literally means Ireland the Free, and I think he'd seen Braveheart or something, and felt that call of Freedom!

(*Switches back to Scottish or English*) So my Dad first went to Egypt when he was three.

He didn't speak Arabic at the time and would be teased by his cousins would for having a funny accent. But within months, (*Arabic accent*) just as he was learning to speak Arabic, (*switches back*) my grandfather was arrested.

One of my Dad's earliest memories is being taken to visit his Dad in prison. Because he was so young, maybe three and a half, they let him through the barrier to sit on his Dad's lap. With the memory of being held tight by his father, he has this image of looking out through the prison bars at his mother and grandmother.

Something like this, maybe?

> *The scene of going to prison is recreated, somehow embodied. The child version of a father greeted by his father, who takes him in his arms, and holds him before placing him on his lap. This scene is given time to be remembered. The grid of the prison bars and the hug, will become motifs.*

During his imprisonment, a fellow cellmate painted this image of my grandfather as a political prisoner. It is dated two days after my Dad turned four, in 1956. It hung on the wall throughout his childhood, and mine.

12 years later, my father has his first experience of being arrested, and by 1975 he's been to prison five times, so my grandfather sits down with him and says,

(*In Arabic*) Boss habiby, enta law ma safertesh, mesh hatetkharag w omraq haydee3. Fa seeb el balad, roo7 kamel derastak, we ba3dein e3mel el enta 3ayzo.

13

*Subtitled: "**Look, habiby, if you don't leave, you'll end up without a degree and have your life stolen. Leave the country, finish your studies, then do what you want.**"*

Bas ya Baba, ana mesh 3ayez ahrab.

*Subtitled: "**But Baba, I don't want to run away.**"*

W howa el sign ahsan?

*Subtitled: "**You'd rather go to prison?**"*

La2.

*Subtitled: "**No.**"*

Matkhafsh. Ma feesh had beyehrab.

*Subtitled: "**Don't worry. No one escapes.**"*

And so my parents get married and go to Iraq in 1975, such is the world that was.

Two years later there are bread riots in Egypt.

(This could be video.)

Sadat, Egypt's president, had signed a deal with the World Bank that stipulated an austerity programme. Neoliberal deregulation began, and subsidies on basic foods were removed. The price of bread and rice sky-rocketed. And so the poor rioted.

As a well-known trouble-maker my father was on the list of people to be rounded up automatically. Had he returned, he would have been taken to prison straight from the airport, and most probably there would be no me, which means no this.

(A beat registering nowhere as somewhere. Summoning the thread, or the ghost.)

(*Gestures to the air and reaches for a pen*) With the stroke of Sadat's pen, another child of neoliberalism is born.

—

Image sequence of Neoliberalism—to Coincidance *by Handsome Dancer, the lyrics resonating, as with all the songs.*

A timeline of neoliberal motifs and figures, interspersed with images/ video of Aalam dancing in hospital to the same song.

Images of Sadat, Thatcher, Reagan, Pinochet, Den Xiaoping, alongside images of protest, and various graphs and statistics about wage growth, inflation, global inequality, climate etc.

And then one day, it happened
They went off to the world
They went on to a journey
Idolized by the boys and girls

They learned so many lessons
In all the foreign lands
But no matter where they wound up
They never stopped the dance

Then turned to face each other
It was just happenstance
That these two men would meet that day
And do that faithful dance

Wow, you can really dance
Wow, you can really dance

He went
He went

They said, "We've both been dancing all this time
What a coincidence!"

*Ends on the card, "**But what the $£€¢ is Neoliberalism?**"*
Followed by an internet meme crib:

Neoliberalism 101

"Neoliberalism is a form of capitalism in which the state deregulates the economy, destroys unions, decreases taxes on the rich and corporations, and defunds public goods, while repressing and policing the poor, particularly people of color."
Joseph M. Schwartz

Actively favors big business interests and the wealthy.

Removes protections of labor law.

Guts welfare, eliminates social services.

Police power, incarceration are instruments of social policy.

Free trade policies empower corporations to seek cheap labor and resources.

Military force used to repress opposition abroad as well as at home.

Pass it on.

—

Me and Aalam met in November 2011.

During the moment I call the 'Fork in the Road', when maybe things could have gone differently.

And I guess the question is, why did we meet? Was it just coincidence?

What legacies bring us to each other?

Part of my experience of revolutions is that they force people out of themselves.

Before the revolution, Aalam used to produce anonymous videos against the regime and post them online. He became an online phenomenon. But he didn't tell a soul what we was doing.

But come 2011, he could work in the open.

The war of images forced us to find our allies.

Create a point in which to gather, and people come.

Hold the space for long enough, they start to come up with ideas, and organise themselves.

That's the basic principle of how we and other made Mosireen.

A collective of citizen media-activists, who with time become one of the major sources of images and video of the Egyptian revolution.

(An image of Tahrir Cinema, with a projector)

And there I am, in another world, or is it this one?

But of course change isn't linear. There come moments when forces collide and you have to defend the future you want.

In October 2011 a massacre of 29 people takes place outside the Egyptian Radio and Television Centre, Maspero. People are run over with tanks, and the army claims that protestors had stolen the tanks and run themselves over.

(Video of tank pauses at the moment just before the crush)

The Egyptian army would never do this to its own people.

Would it?

(A tear gas cannister, or flare is released—an object that smokes up the space, and creates a moment of embodiment.)

Within weeks the streets erupt into the second wave of the Egyptian revolution, Mohamed Mahmoud. Thousands return to demand an end to military rule.

What I call the 'Fork in the Road'.

(Images/Video—then paused)

A moment we didn't win.

A few years later, just as I was returning to London after the Brexit vote, I met an artist called Aura Satz. She was doing a project on sirens.

I tell her I have a story about the hundreds of wailing ambulances that treated the dying and injured, their sirens looping over each through the night. From it she makes this recording which I play to Aalam next time I'm in Egypt. He shut the windows and the balcony, and turned the volume up.

(Guttural trumpet siren created by Mazen Kerbaj starts playing. The text is from the recording)

The sound…uh… got to me. And I remember it. I can kind of still hear it.

(As the recording plays, a lamp of some kind is constructed, and the performer's full body becomes a turning twisting siren, like a dervish —OR some kind of light event is constructed out of this, a kind of visual summoning of its own—with space to think and find yourself.)

The siren itself. The consistency of the sound was much more than itself.

It wasn't the ambulance anymore it was the sound of the persistence of that act of violence. It wasn't a sound to call you in. It was a sound to push you away.

Because it wasn't the persistence of the sound of struggle, which in a way it could have been.

It's the densest moment, conceptually, I think, in terms of everything that's been going on in the world subsequently. It's the place from which I unfurl most of my readings and metaphors or whatever.

Between those range of events and images and collapse of narratives, uh… um… we have that window, that kind of, that narrow frame, to a complete other possibility.

I try to keep alive my relationship with my version of the emergency.

That's why it's important to return, and keep returning to the points where you felt a different thread, a different possibility. That for me is the spirit with which you try and keep another future possible.

—

When I played it to Aalam in his flat in Cairo, Egypt was in a state of authoritarian freeze. He broke into tears, and then immediately picked up a pen and drew a door on his white walls.

(Something on the screen, or something happens to the walls)

"We should have died there, Khalid. We should have tried harder. All of us."

—

(*In a Scottish accent*) OK, enough already. It's all got so bloody serious!

(*Back to English*) A little game for our inner children.

Please open the envelope that was given to you when you entered.

In it you will find two pieces of paper and a mirror, for now, just take out the mirror.

In the midst of 2013, when things got really bad, in a flash of madness me and Aalam decided to start a campaign called Masmou3.

Basically things were so dark, and curfew created such overwhelming silence, that we couldn't believe we were so alone, and politically atomised.

Cairo—a city that normally sounds like this—

Had become like this—

I'd been to Istanbul, earlier that year, and witnessed that every day at 8 o'clock those that couldn't go to protests, would make sounds or flash their lights on and off for five minutes.

I showed Aalam a video.

(Video of overwhelming lights and sound in Istanbul plays)

Do you think we could do that here?

And so in our madness, we did. And a range of equally mad people joined us, making noise every night at 9 o'clock—taking videos and sending tweets.

Of course things ended up getting complicated. Aalam's house was raided and he was arrested, then released after a crazy international chorus of solidarity got him out.

But he ended up blindly wiping hard drives in the frenzy that followed his freedom. So much of his work gone. Such was the price.

Point is, here, we're safe.

And so in the spirit of that madness, I am going to ask questions. And I'm going to ask you to reply by rumbling your feet.

Can we check what a full audience sounds like?

And if I speak in a Scottish accent, can I get even more?

Right, let's just pull out all the stuff that's hidden in this room between us. You've got quite a lot of me already. Let's find out who we are?

If you were born in the UK, please…

If you were born outside the UK, please…

Interesting.

If both your parents were born in the UK, please…

If both your parents were born outside the UK, please…

And if it's only one…

OK.

If you've been to any Arab countries, please…

If you've been to Egypt, please…

Palestine…?

Israel….?

Oooooh.

Gaza…?

If you've eaten something today that was grown outside this country, please…

If you've eaten something that you know was grown in this country, please…

If you know someone who's been to prison, please…

If you've ever been arrested, please…

If you love the current government, please…

If you think things need to change, please…

Continues both humorously and pointedly, with some improvisation— it's also a listening game. Could involve images. Could involve a moment with specific audience members… At the right moment

*energetically… Ends with Theresa May's - "**And if you believe
you're a citizen of the world, you're a citizen of Nowhere.**"*

—

Thank you, Theresa.

OK. Next. (*The below is improvised, the text is just for reference*)

Please take out the rectangular piece of paper, and leave the
square one.

One of the delights of having kids is just watching the ease with
which they pick up a colouring pencil and feel the freedom to
draw whatever it is they want, then say, right, finished, done.

But then it comes. For most of us, it comes.

No, I'm terrible at drawing.

Awful.

I draw like a seven year old.

Apparently, whatever age you stop drawing is the age you will
appear to draw like next time you do. So if you stopped at nine,
next time you draw, you'll draw like a nine year old. And so on.

One of my big childhood regrets is that I stopped drawing. A
teacher said something dismissive to me, and that part of me
froze. I amputated it.

Can you draw?

No I'm terrible at drawing.

Awful. Awful.

When the white walls closed in on me, and everything started to
feel impossible, I sat down and wrote a list of things I wished I
could do and wasn't.

It was a looong list, but on it was drawing. Something ….
possible.

I don't need to be an artist, I just don't want to feel that horrible attack (*machine gun sound again*) when the idea of drawing appears. It's such a familiar attack, maybe if I heal my relationship with it, it will give me more resilience elsewhere.

Is what we tell ourselves is impossible actually impossible. Do we dramatically narrow our paths? Out of... shame, fear?

I searched out a friend.

I just want to learn some principles. I'm sure there's just basic stuff I can learn.

Could you show me how you draw? Just anything.

And I looked at the page and ... (*holds the moment of terror. Really....?*) drew like the last time I'd drawn, age 13.

Fuck it was hard, and bloody awful...

But then suddenly the improvement became rapid. I wasn't producing art but I was producing something I had told myself was impossible, gone from this lifetime.

And so I kept going.

One of the practices I've developed and love is the blind self-portrait.

You look at yourself, and without looking at the paper, draw. And only look when you're finished.

I do it at crazy moments, when there's three or ten minutes that are apparently pointless.

A gentle dialogue with the impossible.

Sometimes it results in something I like more.

Sometimes something I like less.

This was the first.

I was sitting down to do a first attempt at a self-portrait, and I spent so long trying to work out how to sit and where to sit and what to do with the light, that it became too late, and I thought to myself I can't go to sleep without drawing anything.

What have I got to lose?

It opened a path.

They ended up sitting together.

(*Shows blind portrait next to charcoal portrait*)

I'm still learning.

If you're willing, using the mirror, in the next few minutes draw yourself. The only rules are, don't look at the paper until you've finished, and try not to take your pen off the paper.

You might not be comfortable doing so now, in which case feel free to do it at home, or some other time that may come.

You can keep it to yourself, or share it outside, online, or bring it onstage.

I will do mine at the same time.

(*Everyone who is willing does so.*

Perhaps there is a sharing. At the very least Khalid shares his. An improvised moment)

—

For me, it is always born of a relationship with my grandfather's portrait in prison.

(*In Arabic*)

Shall I look to you?

No, it's better if you look up. Bit less.

Like this?

Imagine you're looking out, the other side of the road.

(*Beat*)

What?

Nothing.

What?

They thought they could bury us, but they didn't realise we were seeds.

What?

It's written on the wall.

Where?

Over there.

—

In the middle of 2015, I was traveling from Cairo to New York. I was the only person of my profile. A man, in his 30s, with a British Passport, but Egyptian, transiting in London. My city. I had to go to the counter to print my boarding pass for the flight from London to New York. I wasn't allowed to print it in Cairo.

I walk to the United counter—and as I'm approaching—they're not recognising me for playing the lead hijacker in *United 93* —the lady at the counter picks up the phone and before I've opened my mouth, says:

"Mr Abdalla is here—Please wait a moment."

I wait.

A well-set blonde US border force lady walks towards me from the distance. I can still see her. She takes my passport.

(*We feel her presence*)

She asks about every stamp. I've been to Morocco.

Turkey.

Jordan.

Qatar.

Lebanon.

Syria.

Afghanistan.

(*American accent*) "Why?"

Almost every answer is..

Um, I was filming.

"The United Arab Emirates?"

That was for a film festival.

"Why are you going to the States?"

Um, another film festival.

I've had to list some of the people I know there. So she asks me…

"How long have you known them?"

20 years, ten years.

"How do you know them?"

Um, school, or you know, friendships from projects.

"Why do you know them?"

(*holds an awkward moment, and laughs*)

Why do I know them?

> *Silence is held, with clarity that the question has to be answered.*

> *And out of the violence of the question, we enter a sequence delivered to the border guard that could never have been said, gradually ramping up.*

Um, well, there is of course no single answer, but there are threads to follow.

My parents wouldn't have ended up here, had life been better in Egypt.

And when you trace the origins of the mess of problems in our region, you can't tell its story without spiralling back to Britain, and the legacies of European colonialism. Right?

The world of staggering inequality we live in has a history that underlies the dynamics of so much movement. And sure, I'm Egyptian, but I'm also what you see me as—an Arab.

Britain and France ruled the Arab region for the entirety of my great grandparents' lives on both sides, and until my grandparents had my Mum and Dad.

In the case of some countries it was over 130 years, like Algeria. In others, like Palestine, it was closer to 'just' 30 years.

Any of the people around us who come from a country with a colonial legacy will no doubt have their own version of this story.

The surnames of giant statesmen orient our landscapes and conflicts in ways that are unimaginable.

Just say the words Rhodes, Balfour, Sykes, Picot, and you have a whole series of intersecting histories unfold for us.

So the story goes, after weeks of frustrated deliberation about how to divide the Ottoman part of the region after the First World War, Sykes had a brain wave that has shaped destinies.

(This extracted text from government minutes performed)

"Mr. Balfour: At first sight it looks as if that would weaken and not strengthen our position in Egypt... What do you mean to give exactly?

Mr. Sykes: I should like to draw a line from "e" in Acre to the last "k" in Kerkuk.

(Map shown, perhaps with line drawn or animated)

'A' went to France. 'B' to Britain.

And now we're here.

In the case of Egypt, Britain was the de-facto ruler for 70 years.

The occupation began in 1882, the year my great grandfather was born.

So the story goes, he was hidden as a baby under the table when British troops passed through his village.

(Perhaps audio of what the moment might have sounded like)

His name—Abdalla—is my surname.

In a story that ties together histories of capitalism and empire through cotton, slavery and the Suez Canal, you get to a man named Cromer.

He was the person put in charge of restructuring Egypt's economy, and securing the flow of Imperial trade through the Suez Canal. He arrived straight from India.

History doesn't repeat itself, but it rhymes.

The pretext for Egypt's occupation was the suppression of a revolutionary movement. What we would now call austerity measures had been imposed, and half of Egypt's tax revenues started flowing out of the country while the poor struggled to feed themselves.

It's a story not dissimilar to the bread riots of the 1970s that resulted in me being born here.

And it's repeating itself now.

But start asking Cromer the kind of questions I'm used to being asked at borders and you reveal an anti-biography that touches everyone.

For his real name was Evelyn Baring. His grandfather founded Barings Bank—the second oldest merchant bank in history.

What they called 'the sixth great European power." A great deal of its wealth was built on the back of the slave trade.

In 1802, Barings Bank brokered the largest land sale in history, known as the Louisiana Purchase. The barely 15-year-old US government, acquired the land from the French. Napoleon wanted to finance his war efforts. The United States of the time, doubled in size.

(A map showing the huge scale of the Louisiana Purchase)

Look at this map again, and you'll see that what they 'sold' was not French-owned land, but the 'right' to dispossess the indigenous peoples who had lived there for thousands of years.

The profits flowed into the city around us now—London, and if you're from... where are you from?... Colorado? Well, his family made some part of you too. And here we are.

Evelyn was born in a little town on the coast of Norfolk, called Cromer.

Cromer is the name by which he's known in Egypt, because in memory of his childhood, it is the official title he gave himself when he was knighted.

I went to Norfolk as it happened one of the weekends we were released from lockdown.

I couldn't help myself. I looked up his birthplace, Cromer Hall. It turned out, you could park right outside in the country lane and look at it.

As I walked round the town, reading his name, but really the town's name, everywhere, I wondered if I was the only Egyptian here. But I could also see in the town the kind of struggling economy that we've come to associate with the Britain that needs 'levelling up.'

Not too far from Cromer, is the port of Felixstowe, Britain's largest port, and the sea seemed to be carrying some of the history of British Imperial trade.

I'd been reading about the history of the container, and how it underpins globalisation.

Of course it's all in my mind…

I decided to dig further, and came across an article.

But it wasn't about Evelyn Baring Sr, the governor of Egypt, it was about his youngest son, Evelyn Baring Jnr—who was governor of Kenya in the 1950s when a network of prisons and concentration camps incarcerating 1.5 million people was built to suppress the Mau Mau Rebellion.

Tens of thousands, if not hundreds of thousands were killed.

And then it turns out that Evelyn Baring Jnr is the grandfather of Mary Wakefield, none other than Dominic Cummings's wife.

I dig into the Barings family tree, and British aristocracy being what it is, I discover that Diana, Princess of Wales, is a distant relative of the Earl of Cromer. OK, fine. So's Churchill.

I'd recently been cast as Dodi Fayed in *The Crown*.

But then I discover that the Spencers, Diana's family, used to be Earls of Wimbledon, where I grew up, and my parents' house is on their ancestral lands.

At which point the only words I had left were "fuck off."

Fuck off!

Why do you know them…?

(*Returns to the reality.*) Why do I know them…

I guess because they like me?

   (*Bursts into sound that takes over*)

—

WHO ARE YOU? WHERE ARE YOU?

LAND. BORDERS. MOVEMENT.

Passport.

A line is created, at whatever angle. A line that is a border, a line for the prison visit, a threshold.

Each time it's crossed. A destination. A name. An evocation. A timeline. There might be a journey in how it's crossed.

(The text in this scene is pre-recorded or projected. Not spoken. A choreography found for the body.

This images in this section bear witness.)

First time in Egypt. 2 years old. Father held overnight.

Jump. Jump. Jump. Jump. Every time we visit, a different count. 4 hours. 6 hours. 2 hours. 4 hours.

Around the age of four I'm allowed to cross the line to give him a bottle of water. *(Does so.)*

Why does your father do these things?

When I turn 18, it starts for me. 1 hour. 2 hours.

Palestine. (Shhhhhht) May 2000. First time entering the West Bank. 6hrs.

Passport: British.

Name: Khalid Hossam Ibrahim Abdalla.

Where are you actually from: Egypt.

Father's Name: Banquo.

Mother's Name: Medea.

Married or Divorced

Paternal Grandfather's name: Ibrahim.

Maternal Grandfather's name: Mohamed.

Paternal Grandmother's name: Alia.

Maternal Grandmother's name: Yousreya.

How many children?

Their names.

Where they live.

Reason for travel.

Where will you be staying?

Names.

The floor turns into designations that will shift. Three lines.

Area A? Area B? Area C?

Area A—Full Palestinian Control.

Area B—Palestinian and Israeli Control

Area C—Israeli Control.

At first all three lines, divide the space equally. And then proportional to the land distribution.

Area A: 18% (including Gaza); Area B 22%; Area C 60%.

At each crossing. Passport. ID.

The floor gradually turns into a grill, a bit like the one from earlier.

Hebron—2000—Area C

Population 120,000 Palestinians. 450 Settlers.

I visit the Ibrahimi Mosque, namesake of my grandfather.

Walking through the market.

Palestinians below. Settlers above. Curfew controlling who can walk when.

I also visit Gaza.

2001—9/11

2002—Me and Cressida have our first conversation about Israel and Palestine. (Shhhhhhh, don't talk about Israel and Palestine.)

2003—Operation Shock and Awe.

New York. 2005. First time after 9/11, to film *United 93*. First time I'm finger printed.

(Universal - bo ba ba ba, bo ba ba ba baa, brum brum)

2008. Second time visiting Palestine.

The Wall.

Second time in Hebron.

The market has been shuttered into a ghost town. Walls inside the city.

(Holds the pose from 2008)

Through here to the Ibrahimi Mosque.

On this trip I first learn about Shuhada Street, where the street is segregated.

This side for settlers, Israelis and tourists. The narrow side for Palestinians.

Gaza—no entry. Under siege.

December 2008 —War in Gaza.

Demonstration in Cairo—I'm arrested while filming. Released same day. British Passport.

2009 —Cressida travels to Israel and Palestine for the first time. Because she's born in Abu Dhabi, she's asked if her father ever slept with an Arab woman. They didn't ask about me.

2010—For the first time in her life, my grandmother is finger-printed in Egypt to get her visa to the UK.

2012—War in Gaza.

2014—First retina scan. Qatar.

2014—War in Gaza.

LA 2015—"I'm sorry you had to wait so long. Don't worry, it's just your name."

2015—Palestine. Film Festival.

Video from Tunnel.

Gaza—Still under siege.

2016—Back home, in London. Where I grew up. Where my children are born.

2016—Alia, my other grandmother, sick with Alzheimers, who no longer knew her own name, has to be finger-printed by authorities in our house to renew her visa.

The visa was denied. Until we took the Home Office to court, and won.

Oyster Card: See it. Say it. Sort it.

Don't see it. Don't say it. Don't sort it.

2020: Stay home.

2021: Stay Alert.

2022. Hands. Face. Space.

2023: First facial recognition AI Gun installed on Shuhada Street in Hebron.

2023.

(Images of October 7, ending with Led by Donkeys *February 2024 video with 11,500 children's clothes laid out on Bournemouth beach, the camera reaching up into the sky)*

—

We have a moment to recalibrate in which all we hear is the sea.

And then we see it, mighty in power. A sea event. Like the Siren.

Breath.

Goes to take photo, and then takes it to an audience member to pass around.

This is a photo of my parents in London in 1974, before they were married, before they went to Iraq, before they had an inkling that London would become their home.

We like to think of ourselves as one body, in one place, in one time, regardless of the provenance of what we eat, regardless of the fuel that give us light and motion, regardless of the materials of our existence and what it costs to main their flow.

But while we have one body, we are not one body. At least that's what I believe.

The photo going round was taken in Trafalgar Square, which seven months ago became the place that led to my first police interrogation.

What is it about certain spaces that gathers our energy?

Trafalgar. Tahrir. Taksim. Republique. The Lincoln Memorial. Syntagma.

The Paris we've come to know was built to suppress revolutionary insurrection. The long boulevards were built for military sight lines, and the etoiles were designed to ensure multiple supply lines and points of attack.

Downtown Cairo, where I live in Egypt, was built on Haussman's model, known as the Paris of the Nile. Tahrir is its major etoile.

The debt incurred to build it, created the circumstances for Britain's occupation.

When it came under attack and we were weaponless, it was the literal ground under our feet with all its histories that we had to dig up and throw to protect us. Fighting on multiple fronts, exactly as Haussmann intended.

(Sound & video of battle. Another embodied moment. Perhaps a section explored with contact mics)

At first, I found myself wanting to adhere fully to non-violence.

Then I started digging up the street.

Then the stones needed transporting to the battle front.

At which point I ask myself what's the difference between digging up the stones and throwing them.

And so I throw as best I can.

Until one of those stones came back and hit me on the head...

(Sound stops/shifts)

...giving me a scar.

Each semi-circle is an image of seven generations.

Which is to say that the ground under our feet belongs to all of us.

(Sound reverses)

If you take my blood. This is the picture it gives you.

And if we look a little closer.

(We see Khalid's DNA mapped onto Palestine and the Levant)

There but for the grace of God, go I.

Map this onto Cressida, my partner of 23 years. The person closest to me in love and thought.

And you get this.

Otherwise known as this.

(Nawar and Aya. Our kids. Perhaps we watch some of their first experience of a carwash, dialogue a mix of Arabic and English.

Squeals of delight and wonder at encountering the world)

Five generations back—a stone's throw—their family line includes, we discover, colonial tailors who had a shop on Trafalgar Square.

(Perhaps we watch video of the cars passing by)

They probably out-fitted Cromer, and many others on their way to the breadth of the British Empire.

Where it was is the Pret A Manger. We went there on an anti-Brexit march and bought mango chunks for my kids, none the wiser of the family connection.

Inside us all is a landscape of struggle.

With each generation a search for agency and liberation.

(Video)

But how?

I got my first post-Brexit European stamp on my way to visit Aalam in Paris, after he'd been diagnosed with cancer.

Pancreatic cancer, for those who don't know, is one of the swift ones.

It's almost always diagnosed late. It appears to be a digestive issue. Maybe heartburn. And by the time the tumour is picked up, it's already metastasised. Average life expectancy becomes six months to a year.

Click.

Everything in your life is in relief.

Aalam's first love—painting—became the territory of his creative life.

A stream of images poured out of him, and he created a semi-fictional archive.

Images that he'd drawn in the past, mixed in with images from his memory of those years, dated the same, as if he were a forger of his own paintings.

So much of his work had been wiped on those hard drives after his arrest.

Still, in balance to his looming death, life poured out of him. Searching for a language of witness.

The exhibition he was living for came to pass, and the hospital gave him leave to take us, his friends on a tour. It was a collection of photos that he photoshopped, of tyrants caught in intimate moments, seeming benign. He worked on them while he was hospitalised.

The collection was acquired and gifted to a museum. He wrote me a message saying—"My biggest, unspoken wound has healed. I have healed, Khalid."

He had always burned bright, but under this light, you had to look on in admiration, asking a simple question:

"What would life be like if we lived every day in the knowledge that it might be our last?

What would you say? What would you do? How could we be different?"

Memento Mori.

Even for his funeral, he asked that we dance. And we did.

And so watching his example, what spirit would you bring to each day left, and insist on finding, no matter the darkness?

Play.

(Goes to table and starts folding a paper dove…)

I used to hate the symbol of the dove.

I find the cliché idea of peace really oppressive. The wish that we could all just get along, feels like a way of saying, I want everything to stay as it is, just removing the violence without actually confronting what causes it.

Peace, alone, risks making invisible the core injustices that underlie the way things are, and why some people reach a point where they will risk everything for change.

And so, I lean towards: No justice No peace.

Genocides do not happen without the poison of seeing others as less than human being endemic in the dominant culture, flattening others' stories and traumas, into stereotypes and tropes.

There is a challenge I always feel when I talk about Palestine, in this language, and so on this side of the world, about how I make space for understanding that Jewish trauma, whether in the Holocaust, or on October 7th, has to be acknowledged amid some charge that if I attune to seems to send a message that expressing grief over Palestinians is in conflict with the humanity we can all agree you must have if you honour the Holocaust.

Because only a monster would deny that the Holocaust was one of the most horrific events in history.

And yet to deny the genocide of Palestinians, to deny the apartheid, to deny the 58 years of occupation, the four wars in 17 years of siege in Gaza and what that does to a people who are the children and grandchildren of those ethnically cleansed at the beginning of this 77 year Nakba, now displaced five, six, seven times while bombed from the sky and fucking shot at while starved into the edge of famine, is fucking fine. It's the language of our political class as they become more and more unaccountable, more and more authoritarian, more and more fascist, until when?!

And then you start to realise that the exceptionalising of any one group's grief is a form of supremacy. Building a country on that idea and trying to shape a region on the supremacy of one group's grief or wellbeing over another, whether with European colonialism or Israeli settlers, will always pave the way to injustice, because without equal rights you will never have peace. You will only have racism and apartheid.

When I first did this play we were in a world in which I could understand how the vortex of polarising thoughts about how to hold Jewish grief in the wake of October 7th while looking aghast in the early days of a live-streamed genocide could warp moral clarity, if you felt you didn't know enough, and how that lingered. But now, because we can acknowledge the scale of children killed, there is barely any controversy left in saying that Israel has become the perpetrator of a genocide armed and enabled by the same governments and politicians responsible for looking after our schools and hospitals. Reckoning with where that sits in all of us, and what this genocide in Palestine has revealed about the world we grew up in, is the path to finding my dove.

This dove that I find so hard to hold in a world in which every day I wake up to images that break me, in which for my entire life I have been trained to accept the unrelenting slaughter of Arab bodies, while doing something about that is treated as the kind of thing that could end a career or put you in prison, rather than a pathway through justice to the peace I hold as dear as anyone, because however I'm seen out there, I am also just another human who wants to thrive in dignity, and the safety to play.

Because this is the inheritance of the child that runs into our arms.

Bringing light, and a world to live for through the storm.

Out there my dove has nowhere to land.

But in here, for whatever reason it is that gathers us, it can just about appear.

If it can do so, then perhaps some part of it can leave these doors with you and begin something out there that is amongst us here.

I have to believe in that.

(*Scottish*) Whether it's for the children we have inside us, (*English*) or the children in our collective care.

The dove, sent out again.

Searching for somewhere to land.

From the distance—Music & Mirror Ball—Destination Calabria —*Dance—with a coda of images*.

END

ALSO AVAILABLE FROM SALAMANDER STREET

All Salamander Street plays can be bought in bulk at a discount for performance or study. Contact info@salamanderstreet.com to enquire about performance licenses.

TRADE by Ella Dorman-Gajic
ISBN: 9781914228865

Exploring the currency of female bodies in an underground world, Ella Dorman-Gajic's Trade powerfully pulls into question the archetype of the "perfect female victim" by examining the psychology of a morally complex protagonist.

CLASS by Scottee
ISBN: 9781913630010

This is a book for the middle class, those who didn't grow up in poverty. Scottee uncovers what it is to be embarrassed about where you're from, and why we all get a thrill from watching how the other half live.

DEAD SHEEP by Jonathan Maitland
ISBN: 9781913630782

It is 1989 and a seemingly invincible Prime Minister has sacked Geoffrey Howe, her Foreign Secretary. Tinged with tragedy and comedy, Dead Sheep explores loyalty, love, political morality and Britishness.

these words that'll linger like ghosts till the day i drop down dead by Georgie Bailey
ISBN: 9781914228896

An experimental play about dealing with grief and mental health crises by award-winnning playwright

RICH KIDS: A History of Shopping Malls in Tehran by Javaad Alipoor
ISBN: 9781913630515

A darkly comedic, urgent play that explores the ubiquitous feeling that our societies are falling apart.

www.ingramcontent.com/pod-product-compliance
Lightning Source LLC
Chambersburg PA
CBHW070028110426
42741CB00034B/2687